ALL GRANDMAS GO TO HEAVEN

ISBN: 978-1-915911-72-8
Printed in the United States of America.

Amazon Book Publishing Center 420 Terry Ave N, Seattle, Washington, 98109, U.S.A

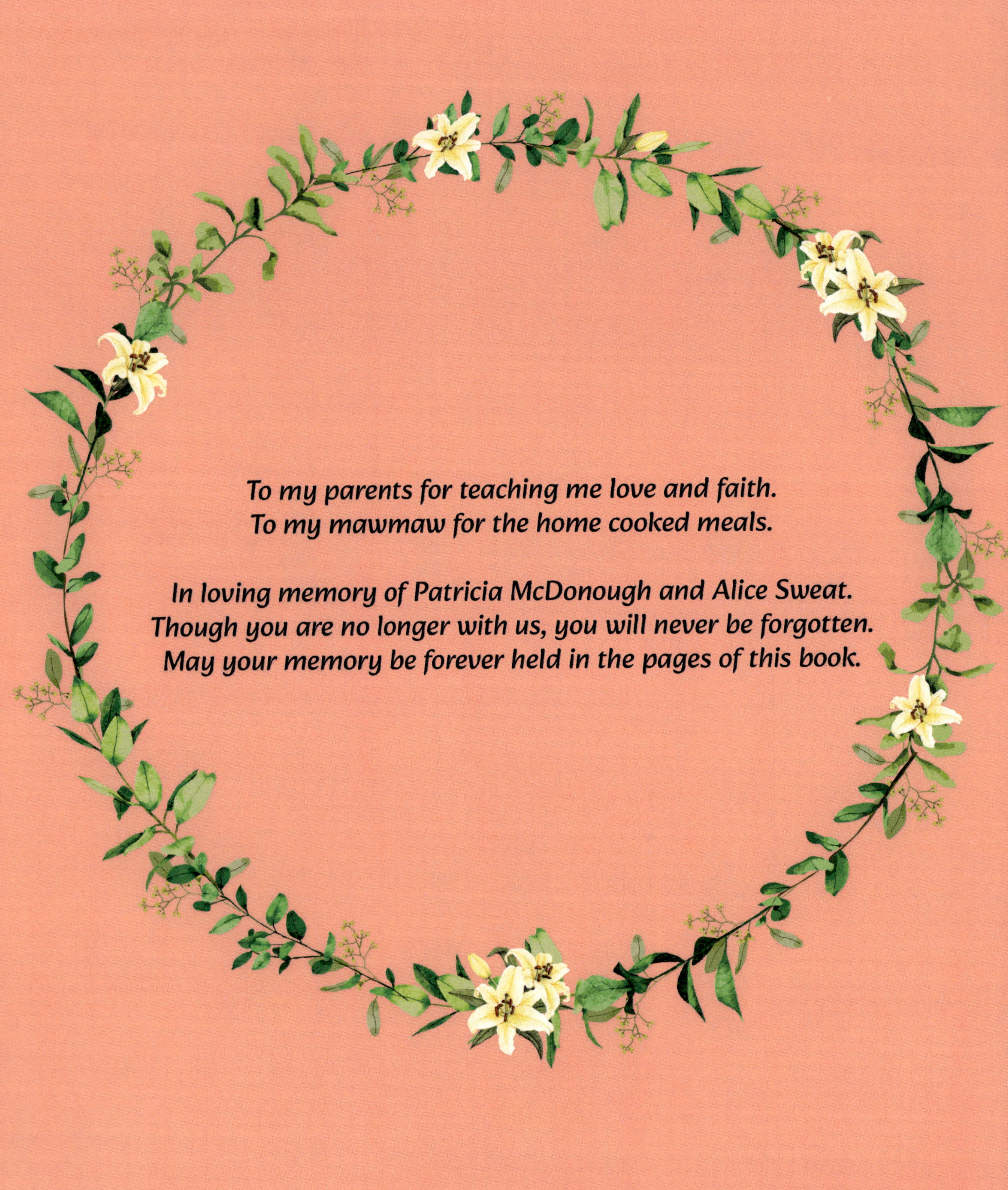

To my parents for teaching me love and faith.
To my mawmaw for the home cooked meals.

In loving memory of Patricia McDonough and Alice Sweat.
Though you are no longer with us, you will never be forgotten.
May your memory be forever held in the pages of this book.

Mommy and Daddy told me
I can't see Grandma anymore.
This made everyone very sad.
Especially me.

I miss playing with grandma
And I miss her hugs and kisses.
She always gave the best of those.

My mommy and daddy cried,
but they told me it's okay.
Because all grandmas go to
heaven and turn into angels.

*And the best thing about angels is
we carry them in our hearts.
So I don't have to go to grandma's
house anymore to talk to her.*

I just lay in my bed
with mommy and daddy
and we whisper to grandma
even though we can't see her.
Grandma is with God now and
they have a lot of fun.

He takes away her pain so grandma
can play in heaven all she wants.
He even lets her see all of her family
who also went to heaven.
She has missed them a whole lot.

Mommy and daddy said one day we will go to heaven and see grandma again, but it won't be for a very long time. Until then, we tell funny stories about grandma and talk about all the times she made us smile and laugh.

Even though I will miss her, I'm lucky
to have grandma as my angel.
Because I know she loves me very
much and is always in my
heart when I need her.

To my grandmother in heaven,
I love you very much.

My favourite memory with my Grandma

PICTURE OF ME AND MY GRANDMA

ABOUT THE AUTHOR

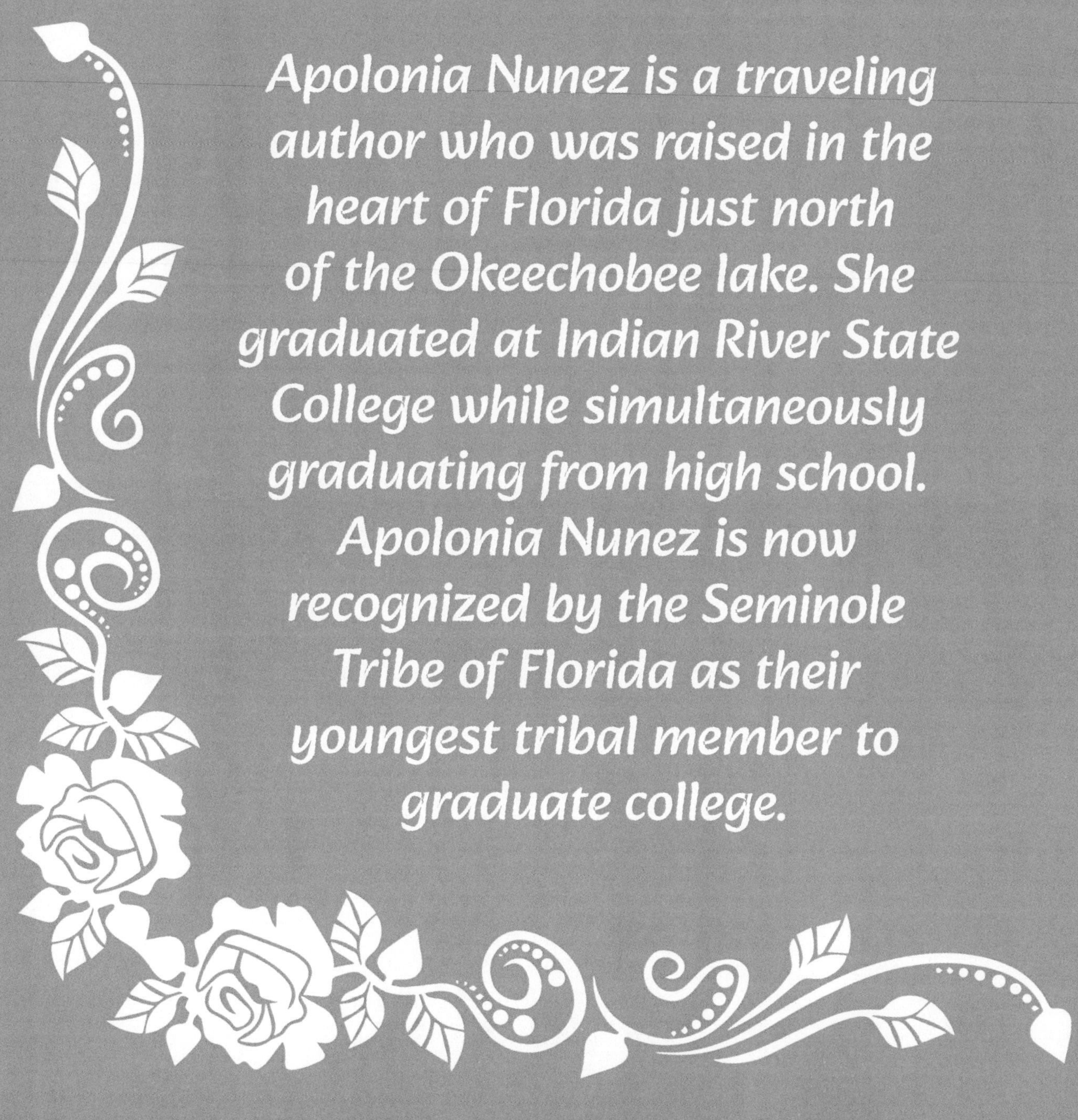

Apolonia Nunez is a traveling author who was raised in the heart of Florida just north of the Okeechobee lake. She graduated at Indian River State College while simultaneously graduating from high school. Apolonia Nunez is now recognized by the Seminole Tribe of Florida as their youngest tribal member to graduate college.

Made in the USA
Middletown, DE
07 September 2023